House for Sale by Owner

Quick Tips on Selling Real Estate

By: Priscilla Greene

I0510823

TABLE OF CONTENTS

Priscilla Greene
PUBLISHERS NOTES

Copyright Act of 1976, the scanning, uploading and electronic sharing of any part of this book without the explicit written consent or permission of the publisher constitutes unlawful piracy and the theft of intellectual property.

If you would like to use material or content from this book (other than for review purposes), prior written permission must be obtained from the publisher.

You can contact the publishing company at admin@speedypublishing.com. Thank you for not infringing on the author's rights.

Speedy Publishing LLC

40 E. Main St., #1156

Newark, DE 19711

www.speedypublishing.co

Cover Artwork: 24 Hr. Designs Ltd.

Editing: Speedy Publishing LLC

Book design: Speedy Publishing LLC

ISBN:

This is a reprint book.

DISCLAIMER

This publication is intended to provide helpful and informative material. It is not intended to diagnose, treat, cure, or prevent any health problem or condition, nor is intended to replace the advice of a physician. No action should be taken solely on the contents of this book. Always consult your physician or qualified health-care professional on any matters regarding your health and before adopting any suggestions in this book or drawing inferences from it.

The author and publisher specifically disclaim all responsibility for any liability, loss or risk, personal or otherwise, which is incurred as a consequence, directly or indirectly, from the use or application of any contents of this book.

Any and all product names referenced within this book are the trademarks of their respective owners. None of these owners have sponsored, authorized, endorsed, or approved this book.

Always read all information provided by the manufacturers' product labels before using their products. The author and publisher are not responsible for claims made by manufacturers.

Priscilla Greene

DEDICATION

This book is dedicated to my family.

INTRODUCTION

So....you'd like to sell your house? Great! Everyone's doing it. But this is your first time and you'll be doing the sale yourself. Nervous? Of course!

The fact is, it's only unnerving because you haven't got a clue about the dynamics of selling a house – your house. It's the one asset you have where you've plunked down your lifetime savings. Now you want it all back!

That equity you were slowly building over these years will come back to you a hundredfold because you've thought about it long enough to realize that there is a handsome profit waiting to be made.

Don't worry! This episode in your life doesn't need to be a drama of horrors. In this book, we've collected important tips for you – the first timer - all 101 of them, in fact.

And when that check finally lands on your hands and the last box has been shipped out of your house to make way for the new owners, it will be exhilarating – more exhilarating than you've ever imagined it to be.

Study the tips. Some you already know, no doubt. But even with 101 or 1001 tips, you'd still need professional advice – you managed to eliminate the real estate agent, but you'll still need your lawyer (or notary) and your accountant.

You need to consult with other professionals as well – like the professional house inspector who can dish out valuable advice about repairs and maintenance.

Priscilla Greene

These tips can help you map out a selling strategy for your house, and when you turn the lock for the last time, you'll come out of the experience wiser. And yes, wealthier, too.

The confidence you gain by getting your feet wet the first time could – who knows? – make you want to do it the second time, and then a third time...and more!

CHAPTER 1- KNOWLEDGE IS POWER

Before Anything Else, Grab a Powerhouse of Knowledge

If you've decided to dispense with a real estate agent to avoid paying those ridiculous commissions, then start thinking like one.

How? Three to six months before your target sale, bone up on home selling strategies. If you have friends or colleagues who've worked in real estate, talk to them, but don't tell them you're thinking of your selling your house so they won't try to convince you to do otherwise.

Ask them about mistakes they've made or mistakes that their relatives and friends have made. Survey the entire landscape. Personal experiences are always an excellent source of knowledge and strategies.

Be a Listener, and Be A GOOD One

Hold casual conversations with at least 3 real estate agents who work in the area where your house is located. Be attentive to what they say about location. It's helpful to know how much your civic address is worth.

While location is the predominant argument in real estate, this rule may not always apply. Perhaps location is the least of your potential buyer's worries. Don't overlook the fact that buyers have typical and unusual reasons for buying a house. Many have jumped into the arena of investment property.

While most people buy houses so they can live in it, there are those who like to play the market and want to make a killing. Sell your house with an open mind. Don't let the factor of location discourage you, or encourage you too much.

Tip 3: Basic rule: don't get locked out of the market because you've overpriced your house!

Continue building up on that knowledge base: make it a daily habit of reading real estate ads every day. Get the average selling price of a house identical to yours.

If you have the luxury of time, you may even want to drive around these houses for sale and judge for yourself whether or not the price they're asking is justified.

Some homeowners have illusions as to what their houses cost. Is the price they ask reasonable, or way out of proportion to the looks and location of the property?

What are the ads saying?

Get a feel of how real estate ads are worded.

- What are the key words and phrases?
- What ads caught your attention?
- Why?
- Does the ad sound credible?
- Does the ad provide adequate information to provoke interest, or does it leave the reader indifferent?

Use these ads as a model for your own.

Play Detective

Do a bit of detective work: try to keep track of real estate ads that appear only a couple of days (house could have been sold in just a matter of days) and ads that seem to be in the paper forever (why can't the advertiser sell? What's preventing him from selling?) This is where wording might clue you into the reasons.

Read And Devour All That You Can!

Build up some more on your knowledge power by visiting your local library, and browsing through books and magazines about real estate in general (and selling homes in particular).

Be on the alert for people who've written about their personal experiences in selling their homes. Being well-informed is still your best weapon.

Realistically Speaking, My House Is Really Worth...

Set realistic goals: if houses like yours in your area are asking for $250,000.00, don't think you could make a lot more just because you have a rose garden and your neighbor doesn't.

Deviating too much from the mainstream can work against you. Don't stop buyers from calling you because your price is way too much the average prices for your area.

Play the Real Estate Game Seriously

Bear in mind that the "no risk, no gain" philosophy may not always work in real estate. Real estate is a smart, serious business. It's better to have brains than guts! Feed your brain with information you will need when you finally do sell your house. Real estate information is not a scarcity. There are thousands of web sites dedicated to real estate. And the library holds a wealth of information on the subject.

Get Only Enough To Get You Started

Priscilla Greene

Too much analysis leads to paralysis. Arm yourself with adequate knowledge and then get moving! Don't let fear or over-confidence immobilize you. If you want to sell your house successfully, fear has no place in the grand scheme of things, nor does arrogance.

CHAPTER 2- KNOW THY AREA/COMMUNITY

Good Schools? But Of Course!

Think about what's special about your community, then conjure up an ad that might attract say, a young couple with school-age children. Find out how many private and public schools there are, and how near are they to your house.

Many times, good schools are the deal clinchers. For young families, schools are a top priority. If the schools in your community have won awards from the private and public sector, or if you hear about any achievements, mention them to your buyers.

It's The Fitness Thing, You Know

Do an inventory of your community's attractions. How many parks, tennis courts are there? Is there a YMCA? All these facilities play a major role in the decision to buy, especially if the husband or wife is a fitness freak.

And What about Concerts and That Kind of Thing

Don't overlook the entertainment factor: how many restaurants and movie theaters does your area have? What about concert halls and other cultural activities? Young couples, especially those with no children, like to eat out often.

They also want the assurance that if they don't feel like entertaining friends for dinner at home, they can go for a concert or a show to spend a relaxing weekend. A very cultural community filled with activities is a huge factor, not only for them, but also for their children.

Priscilla Greene
Will I Fit In The Area?

The ethnic factor: if your area has a strong multi-cultural presence, this might be an attraction for newly arrived immigrants in search of a house. The feeling of wanting to feel "at home" is a strong motivator. You may think it a trivial matter, but buyers do ask if there's a sushi restaurant in the area, or if there are any Jewish Synagogues nearby.

Are there meeting places where members of ethnic communities can mingle and share views, cuisine and stores about "back home"?

Is There A Doctor In The House?

Does your area have a good hospital? What makes that hospital a plus factor? Families that have aging in-laws in tow would like to know if they can get medical help immediately in case of an emergency.

Also, if your local area hospital is known for a particular specialization make sure you let your buyers know.

How Is The Transportation System?

How far are the major highways from your house? Where is the next largest city? How developed is your area's public transportation system? Proximity to a subway station is typically seen by many as a benefit because downtown parking is expensive. This constitutes a great advantage also for teenaged children who attend university downtown.

No Gossiping Allowed!

Are you in friendly terms with your neighbors? If you're selling a condo or a duplex, the next owners are usually curious about what kind of neighbors live in the same enclave.

Show your neighborliness, but don't gossip about the neighbor on your right. Chances are prospective buyers are only interested if the neighbors are quiet or rowdy. They're not interested in your neighbor's alcohol problem.

Help, My Car's Been Snowed In!

How efficient are your city's services? Does the area have enough firemen, snow removal trucks, and garbage collection systems? What about facilities for recycling waste material?

The more you know about your community's services, the better you can capitalize on these selling points.

If either the wife or husband has had a hip fracture, efficient snow clearing by the municipal government is reassuring. Not many cities can say that their snow is cleared on time.

Cavities

Is the city water fluoridated? You'll be amazed at how some parents make a big deal of this. Studies have revealed that cities where the water has been fluoridated have a lower incidence of tooth decay among school-age children.

Perhaps this looks like a minor detail to you, but remember, the intelligent buyer is taking a thorough inventory of the community and its services.

CHAPTER 3- KNOW THY ABODE

Getting To Know Your House...For the Last Time

Okay, you have a good understanding of real estate, you know your community, and now it's time to know your house like the back of your hand.

Every house has a hidden defect or a very visible fault. Take pencil and paper and do a tour, taking down all the weaknesses that can potentially be spotted by buyers when they visit. Go around your house several times to make sure you've covered everything.

You want to discover the defect before the buyer does. Spare yourself some embarrassment. Don't underestimate the buyer's ability to see through walls!

Did You Say An In-Ground Pool?

If your house comes with a swimming pool, mention it! An in-ground swimming pool adds a lot of value to a house.

Make sure the pool is clean and there are no floating algae or fungi when the buyers come knocking at your door.

If there's anything that can be quite disconcerting it's a pool with no water, dead leaves and little creatures floating about, or large cracks in the pool. A pool isn't fun without a heater. Let your buyer know that the pool's heater is working.

Put Romance Back In Their Lives...

If you live in an area with a colder climate – Minnesota for instance -- a fireplace makes a good sell, so don't forget to mention it.

This particular detail can go into the ad, or you can surprise your potential buyer when they come to visit. It's all up to you. Find out what the real estate agents say about fireplaces.

In Florida for example, a fireplace is not something you'd think a house should have, but in upscale, gated communities, families do have nice fireplaces in the living room or basement. Ambiance, that's why.

See, This Garage Door Is Really Simple To Operate!

Check your garage door mechanism and see if it's working properly. You'll want to demonstrate to potential buyers that your garage is in tip top shape.

You may also want to show them your maintenance records (garage doors usually need to be inspected and lubricated once every two years, depending on how recent your garage door and mechanism are).

I Never Promised You A Rose Garden.

Check your front and back yards. Are they well-kept or do they look like they've been neglected for the last six months? Is your grass healthy and green and well-manicured?

When buyers look for a house, they customarily concentrate on making adjustments inside the house; they understand that part of the house buying process is renovation.

At least they're prepared for this event, but when they see that the outside of the house also needs major attention, they could get discouraged – and dismayed no doubt – to see such an unkempt front yard and backyard.

Priscilla Greene
You'll Have a Roof over Your Head for the Next 25 Years

Make a list of major and minor renovations you've undertaken in the last five years. Keep this list in your pocket so that when you give the house tour, you can mention these renovations.

Things like "my husband and I had the roof changed entirely even before the 25-year period. One thing you won't have in this house is a leaking roof".

Or else: "These kitchen cabinets and drawers were given a face lift only three months ago".

Or perhaps: "We decided to install smoked glass in one part of the kitchen to hold our crystal collection". Then turn on the light of the smoke glass cabinet to show some dramatic effect, the expensive crystal collection and the dim lighting.

Wow, a Home Spa!

Pay attention to the bathrooms. Make sure they have good lighting, squeaky clean faucets and a shiny, sparkling bathtub. A stained bath tub is unsightly.

Hang some of your best linens for the visit. A bathroom that smells and looks clean can be a persuasion point. Count yourself lucky if you have a whirlpool or a large Roman bath.

For couples just recently married, the whirlpool or spa might just bring you closer to finalizing that deal. One thing with house hunters: they start with a budget in mind, but watch how they're easily swayed to stretch that budget a little more when they see amenities that they otherwise would not have thought about previously.

A House That's Safe And Sound

Buyers are likely to ask you about insulation and energy efficiency systems in your house. If you don't know or can't remember, be honest and say so.

However, it definitely would be to your advantage if you can speak knowledgeably about the "inner character" of your dwelling. The old installation materials of older houses were declared a health risk by the US and Canadian governments many years ago, and house builders have switched to safer insulation materials.

Make sure you mention this if you do know, especially if you're dealing with a buyer who happens to be a lawyer.

What? No Hot Water Again?

Many people don't know this, but if you were smart enough to have your water heater checked periodically, say so.

Water heaters, in order for them to work efficiently, have to be inspected regularly. Over time, water heaters get an accumulation of chemicals in the bottom. Even if a new roof costs a lot more than a new water heater, buyers appreciate the present owner's thorough "sense of maintenance" by looking into details that homeowners usually overlook.

Someone Forgot To Look Up The Ceiling...

One real estate agent in Washington DC remarked that she was approached by a couple to sell one of the "cutest houses in the neighborhood".

Priscilla Greene

It had excellent potential – large backyard, nice French bay windows, a second floor landing area that was large enough to accommodate a family gathering, and solid wooden floors.

The only thing wrong, according to the real estate agent, was the entire lighting system. The lamps and chandeliers looked like they were put there since the time of Adam and Eve.

She suggested to the present owners to replace all the lights and to invest in good quality lamps. The cutest house in the neighborhood eventually sold – just three weeks later – for $900,000.00

CHAPTER 4- YOUR MOTIVES FOR SELLING: WATCH OUT FOR THE PSYCHOLOGICAL EFFECT

Why Am I Selling?

You made the decision of selling the house. You went through the motions of going over your house and looking for things to repair.

Before you get to the next step – advertising your house in the paper and by word of mouth - spend some quiet time to yourself so you can gauge your true feelings about why you want to sell your house.

If you have compelling reasons or circumstances that force you to sell, this may affect your position as a seller. As the property owner, you should always be on the driver's seat.

Only you can dictate the terms of sale. If you're emotionally or financially disadvantaged, you may want to put off selling your house until you're 100% convinced that you're ready – emotionally and financially.

Not the Time to Be Fickle...

If your house holds much sentimental value and you feel that parting with it will affect you psychologically, assess how strong your emotional attachment to your house is.

Once the house is sold, there is no turning back. Sale contracts are legally binding. You can't appear at the doorway of the new owners and say, "Sorry, I've changed my mind. I acted irrationally by selling. I want my house back!"

Priscilla Greene
Nostalgia Is a Strong Feeling

You want to sell because you're getting divorced from your husband of 25 years? If you no longer love your husband, but still love your house, think twice about selling.

If the house means that much to you, then perhaps you may want to re-consider. A house is not only a physical structure. It is a refuge, a reservoir of memories of a family that built a future together.

Sell your house if you have to, but if you'll spend sleepless nights regretting the decision to sell, you might be risking your mental health.

I'm In a Bind...

Financially strapped? Many people think of selling their house to acquire much-needed cash. Your house is your only asset and perhaps the only asset that banks will look at if you apply for a loan.

Instead of selling, you may consider the option of using the equity you've built up in your home to apply for a loan. But don't sell just because you need cash. Banks are often willing to give you room to maneuver on your house equity.

My Home Isn't A Hotel!

If you hesitate about selling your house because you want your children to have a place to stay when they visit, remember that you raised them to be responsible, self-sufficient adults.

If you really want to sell your house, this should be the least of your worries. Your grown children can perfectly manage on their own. Your house isn't the Four Seasons!

Listen Up, But Stay With Your Convictions!

Remind yourself that it's your house, so buyers should play by your rules. Don't let some smooth talking buyer convince you that your house isn't worth that much.

You did your homework, so you're the only one who knows what you should be getting for your house. Remember it's the buyer who needs a house, not you. If one buyer is starting to get on your nerves, there are other buyers.

I'm Selling, No Matter What

Banish your fears and emotional ups and downs because they only lead to inaction.

Bolster your self-confidence by constantly saying to yourself, "I want to sell my house, I will sell my house, and I will make money from selling my house". This mantra will guide you and make you stronger as you go through the motions of the eventual sale.

Even Well-Meaning Friends Can Derail You!

Stay focused. Don't surround yourself with friends who like to foretell gloom and doom. "You might regret it," or "There's just too much stress handling the sale yourself, let the experts do what they're best at".

These pieces of advice, no matter how well-intentioned, have no place in your goals. Don't be easily swayed by what your friends or

Priscilla Greene

colleagues tell you.   Refuse to listen to horror stories about meeting the strangest of strangers.

CHAPTER 5- GETTING SERIOUS AND GETTING READY

Time to Go "Pro"

Earlier we provided tips on getting to know your house and going around inside and outside to see what needs to be improved.

Now it's time to closely inspect your home for hidden defects. It's time for a professional inspector. Get him to examine those details that can make or break a deal.

One is the electrical wiring. A fire caused by faulty wiring is serious business. Instead of enjoying the cash from the sale of your house, your hard-earned equity is going towards paying damages and lawyers' fees.

The Radon Test

Experts love to mention the radon test. If you run a radon test in your house, this is a huge plus in the eyes of buyers.

The longer the radon test, the more accurate are its results. High radon levels can be fixed. Always do retests, and provide results to your buyers.

This Isn't a Multiple Choice Test

See to it that the professional inspector or home inspection company you hired provides you with a well written report.

The fill-in-the-blank forms and check boxes type of report may be accurate, but a written, detailed analysis looks better to buyers. It demonstrates to them that you've done your sacred duty as seller.

Priscilla Greene
The Well's Run Dry

Don't overlook details that can jeopardize the sale or put you in an awkward position later.

If you have a well (most homes out in the far country still have wells!), have this inspected. If you have a written report, show this as well to the buyers.

What's that Smell?

If you have a septic system, have a percolation test performed. If repairs are necessary, you either repair them before you sell, or disclose them to the buyers. Don't kill your chances of selling your house because of this detail.

Actually, Now That You Ask…

Show all repairs in a written report to all prospective buyers. This will eliminate unpleasant surprises later that might delay the sale. Disclosing all house defects and problems will help reduce the time or process leading to the final sale.

Non-disclosure can even cause a re-negotiation of the sale price if the buyers discover the defects themselves. If there is anything you don't want, it's being forced to re-negotiate the price down because of non-disclosure of a fact that you were legally required to disclose.

Show That You Mean Business!

When the professionals have done their inspections and all reports are in your possession, make copies. You'll want to have as many copies of each report at arm's length, so you're not scampering around for them at the last minute.

Show buyers that you're acting conscientiously and being considerate of their concerns. This will indicate clearly that you're a serious seller – and a professional one. Make sure the dates are clearly visible on each and every report.

If I Were Buying This House...

After you're satisfied that the professional inspectors did their job correctly, act like one. Take one, long last look.

Put on your eagle eyes, and ask yourself: if I were buying this house, what would I want done or repaired?

Is There An Expert Around?

In terms of repairs and fixes, follow the advice of Bill Effros: there are three categories of things you should fix:

- Legally required repairs;
- Little things that make a BIG difference;
- Big things that make a HUGE difference.

It's The Law, Sir

Fix house problems because the law requires you to. These are usually environmental in nature or hidden hazards that can cause health problems for the buyers and their children. Examples are lead paint and asbestos removal, and harmful insulation material.

You And I Are Different

Little things that make a difference are those tasks or jobs that you've somehow delayed or never got around to doing.

Remember that what may be petty to you may not be petty at all to your prospective buyer. No two people think the same way.

Priscilla Greene

Selling and buying a house are two different perspectives, two different people, and two different mindsets.

Did You Inherit These Doorknobs From Your Grandmother?

Try not to overlook old doorknobs and plates on light switches. If they look lifeless and worn, replace them to liven up the living areas. Try to go for neutral designs.

If your buyers are young, upward mobile professionals, you could go for bolder designs. Make sure that whatever you put on, the buyers can take them off easily should they decide to do so.

That Noise Is Driving Me Nuts!

Has that leaking faucet been bothering you lately? You can be sure that minor things like leaking faucets can make buyers hesitate.

Faucets that have been leaking for some time demonstrate a homeowner's negligence regarding basic maintenance.

Is This Door Going To Fall On Me?

Does your house have doors that sag, don't close properly, squeak or have a knob missing?

There are beautiful ready-made and custom-made doors in your local home centre, so why don't you pay them a visit; get an idea of what kind of doors would breathe life into your house?

So, How Many Insects Do You Have Here?

hat about broken screens that have ugly-looking holes gaping at you and your visitors? A simple thing such as broken screens can be a huge turn off so show consideration for your buyers by taking care of these minor fix-its.

For You or the Buyer

Some experts say that little repairs that can potentially annoy you or your buyers must get fixed.

Getting small, minor jobs done will help increase your chances of selling your house.

But getting big things fixed, they say, will only mean profits for the contractor and buyer, not you. This is a matter of personal opinion.

If you take integrity and professionalism to heart, you can proceed with the big repairs and cough up the expense.

Hold Your Horses!

Here's what some experts are also saying about undertaking major repairs. If it's going to cost you an arm and a leg and substantially reduce the sale price of your home, think twice.

For example, your house costs $200.000.00 in the market. You're thinking of selling it for $250,000.00 – to make a neat little profit of $50,000. Repairs will cost you $30,000.00 that reduces your profit by $20,000. Are the major repairs worth that measly profit?

Crunch some figures before you undertake those major renovations.

I Wish You Hadn't Done That...

Undertaking major renovations may come out of the goodness of your heart, but have you ever thought of looking at the other side of the coin?

What if the potential buyers don't particularly like the renovations you've done, and would have preferred to renovate the house themselves?

When an individual goes out looking to buy a house, that individual is not just buying a physical piece of property but is also thinking of making his future house an extension of his personality and his lifestyle.

So if you're thinking of renovating your house before selling to make it look more presentable, those good intentions may backfire. That's why it's always good to gauge a buyer's plans about your house when he/she first makes contact.

Bring In a Contractor

Some people actually think it's a good idea to bring in a contractor to have a look at their homes after the professional inspection.

Because they know their business inside out, some contractors specialize in preparing homes for sale, and can tell you what should be fixed and what should be left alone.

They can help you save precious dollars. Show them all of the inspection reports. With the contractor's opinion and the home inspection reports in your possession, you should be able to decide what to fix and what not to fix.

Chapter 6- Letting the Word Out: "I'm Selling my House!"

Get The Word Out!

Okay, you've had your house inspected and you've done your own inspection. It's time to let the word out.

You can announce the sale of your house through word of mouth or putting an ad on your paper.

Do an experiment: tell your colleagues at work that you're selling your house. Make a note of the questions they ask. Their questions can serve as an accurate indication of what prospective buyers are also likely to be asking you.

Reach Out Far And Wide!

Your announcement can be published in the national and local community paper. The more people you reach, the more prospects you have. You may also announce in trade papers that are published by real estate associations or the housing authority.

Use as many resources as you can. You have no idea how much more successful you will be in selling when there is a larger audience involved.

You may be slightly inconvenienced by the number of inquiries you'll get, but if you want to sell that house in a hurry, it's a question of statistical proportions.

The more you spread the word around in the media, the more people you reach.

Priscilla Greene
Word Of Mouth Is Just As Powerful As Advertising

Ask your office colleagues to tell their families and friends about your house sale. They may know of people who are moving into the area and looking for homes.

The more colleagues you tell, the more you increase your chances of reaching people you don't even know. After you've told them, follow up after a week and ask if they had any questions about your house that you'd be pleased to clarify. Make it known to them that you're serious about selling, that way they take you seriously and some of them will even want to help you.

Can The Company Help Me?

After you tell your colleagues, speak to the human resources manager of your organization and tell her that if there are executives relocating to your area, you have a house to sell.

You'll never know what the human resources individual can come up with.

Someone may actually be moving to the area to take up a position in your organization; or your human resources manager may have been approached by other human resources professionals from other companies who are desperately looking for houses for their expatriates or returning executives.

Ah, the Old Reliable...The Bulletin Board!

Go one step further: use the public bulletin board to post your house sale. Don't forget to leave tabs with your telephone number that can be torn out of the main sheet so that people can call you or pass them on to their friends.

Post a clear picture in color with your ad on the bulletin board. You know how the saying goes - a picture is worth a thousand words.

Am I Missing The Sugar?

Before you even sit down to word that ad for the papers, think about the ingredients of the recipe for successfully selling of your house.

There are five ingredients you need to have, according to Barb Schwarz, a successful realtor.

Let's take the first ingredient: location. You can't physically uproot your house to take it to a better location. Note that the price of your house must realistically reflect its location.

Have You Been Negligent?

Second ingredient for a successful sale: Condition. Remember that this is where a professional inspector and a thorough personal inspection by you can make a lot of sense. Schwarz said that the upkeep of the property is a crucial factor in obtaining the highest possible price for a home. Price, like location, must reflect a house's condition.

How Much Do I Want?

Third ingredient: Price. This is the # 1 deciding factor in the sale or no sale of a house. There's a belief among real estate circles that a house is really only worth what a buyer is willing to pay a seller to gain ownership of that house.

Price must have a direct correlation to all the other ingredients for a successful sale. Never mind what the listings or other people say.

Priscilla Greene

If your house is overpriced, you won't have any offers, or else it may take a long time to receive offers.

Will The Buyer Ask For Flexibility?

Fourth ingredient: Terms. The more terms you have on the property, the more potential purchasers you reach. Again, the price of your house must reflect the kinds of terms available to purchase it.

Is This A Good Time To Sell?

Fifth ingredient: Market. Market conditions are influenced by key factors such as interest rates, supply and demand of houses in your area, competition and the general state of the economy.

Real estate is a cyclical phenomenon. The beginning of 2000 witnessed a surge in home building. All of a sudden homes were being sold faster than contractors could build them. When there's a real estate boom, this is an excellent opportunity to make a killing!

The Truth Will Come Out...

So keep those five ingredients uppermost in your mind at all times. Now you're ready to word that ad.

Be honest.

Don't say you have a house in excellent condition when your inspection report has a long list of deficiencies and repairs your house will require.

Don't say you have 3 full bathrooms when you really have only two bathrooms and one powder room. A powder room, as we all know, does not qualify as a full bathroom.

Also, don't say that you live in a quiet neighborhood when in fact your house is located near a university campus where you hear students partying all night. If you mention that your house has an alarm system, it better work.

Umm, How Will I Word This Ad?

If you aren't good with words, that is, it's taking you painstakingly long to draft an ad, go with ads placed in the local and regional papers that you FEEL works for you.

This means putting yourself in the buyer's shoes: you read the ad, it makes you curious, and you take down the number. If an ad pleases you or strikes you as effective and persuasive, copy the style and content of the ad.

Another alternative would be to refer back to some of the books you read on successful real estate sales and mull over the model ads.

Can You Just State The Bottom Line Please?

When you're ready to write out an ad, clarity and brevity must be your parameters. If your price is reasonable and realistic and you put the ad in the right strategic places, you'll get at least 20 calls.

Do Your Thinking before Picking up That Phone

Don't do what many people do. They call the classified ads department of their local and regional papers and craft the ad with the person in the other line.

Don't waste time by providing information only while you're on the phone. Instead, figure everything out in advance.

Priscilla Greene

And when we say everything, we mean that by the time you call the classified ads person, you know ahead of time what your ad will look like, what it will say, where to put it, what abbreviations to use and whether or not it should have a border (experts say you don't need a fancy border for your ad to catch the readers' attention).

Bill Effros who sold his house in five days said that you don't need a double column or a fancy border for your ad.

Wait and See

Be careful about how long you want your ad to run. An ad that's been around too long will give readers the impression that your house is not selling because of major problems. It will also tell them that maybe buyers are coming to see the house only to walk away disappointed.

Some experts say a five-day ad is sufficient. If you don't get a sufficient number of serious callers, pull out the ad, wait a few weeks, and start all over again. Review the ad's wording. Perhaps there's something in the ad that doesn't sound right that you didn't notice the first time.

Where Should I Publish?

Put it in two sure places where it will get read. Again, pretend you're the buyer looking for a house. Where would you most likely look? That's the section where you should place your ad.

Your local paper with a small circulation and your regional paper with a much larger circulation should be your target destinations for your ad.

Tip 72: One Is Enough

Buyers often don't really want to buy 4-5 newspapers to look for houses for sale. They'd much rather concentrate on one paper and encircle the ads that could lead to potential visits. They usually go for the paper which is the most popular with the highest number of readers. That's the paper where your ad must also go.

Cyberspace? Do I Really Want Martians Buying My House?

What about placing my ad on the Internet, you ask? If our guess of the human tendency is right, people may look at the Internet for houses for sale, but may not necessarily be serious buyers.

So the Internet for now would be an alternative to traditional newspaper advertising. Just watch people in cafes who are reading the classified ads. They usually mark the paper, circling those ads that they're interested in.

On the Internet, the buyer would either copy contact details by hand or print the ad – this can be cumbersome. At least with the newspaper at hand, people can just toss it in the seat of their cars as they drive off to visit the property, and can look at the ad again, if needed.

Do You Want To Write A House Story? Try The Home Section, Not The Classified Ads

Think twice, even three times before you get that pencil or word processor moving. Avoid flowery words. Avoid expressions like "it will capture your heart", or "a house of your dreams", or "here's a house where you can have many memorable days".

People are not really looking for something to captivate their hearts or memories. They're looking for a real house to live in, for a roof over their heads. The dreams and memories can come later,

Priscilla Greene

but at this point, buyers are only interested in a physical structure that they claim ownership of.

What Should I Say?

Word your ad so that it answers the questions that buyers would want to know: location, the fact that you're selling it yourself (no brokers or agents please), brief description of house, a starting reasonable price.

Mention that you'll take the best reasonable offer, and put your area code and telephone number. These are the only points that buyers are initially interested in. Other details like amenities and extras and true value can be discussed face to face or during a follow-up telephone call.

This Is EXACTLY How I Want It

Bill Effros recommends that your ad should be positioned as follows: location, upper top left and "BY OWNER" right hand side top.

Type of house (condo, duplex, cottage, etc) on the next line.

Brief description of major feature on the following line.

Then your starting price, e.g. "$150,000 or best reasonable offer" on the next line, to be followed by inspection times (e.g. Sat-Sun 10-5).

Last line on low bottom left, the words: "HIGHEST BIDDER", and your telephone number beside it.

Note: your ad is meant to give you as many callers as possible. Details about the property can be provided to them on the phone if they request them.

And to play safe, email or fax the copy of the ad exactly as you want it to appear in the paper. You could be dealing with an ad taker who is taking ads for the first time and may not understand what "flush left" or "flush left" mean.

Screen Calls

If you're a busy person with a full time job, you may want to filter your calls. Before you call the paper to have your ad put, make sure you set yourself up with an answering machine or an answering service.

You don't want to be called in the middle of the night or at meal times to answer questions about your house and be forced to make a visit appointment. With an answering machine, you decide who you want to call back.

You will also be able to tell who the serious buyers are versus the frivolous ones. People who leave their names and numbers and are brief in their message make a good impression.

You want to avoid receiving callers who talk incessantly or ask questions the answers of which are already in the ad.

Be wary of people who also try to negotiate the price down over the phone without even asking to see the property.

This should raise your antennas to the fact that one, they probably can't afford the price to begin with, or second, they can't get their bank to finance that amount.

Add "Or Best Reasonable Offer"

Priscilla Greene

A famous real estate writer says that it's not so much the description of the property that will get you a sufficient number of callers; it is the stated price on your ad.

If it is within their price range, they will call. If not, they'll go on to the next ad. So make sure you don't omit this detail but add, "or best reasonable offer."

It's My Favorite Day of the Week!

Only you will pick the days you want your ad to appear. The approach is to reach as many readers as possible. In the United States, Sundays are when the ads run in the hundreds, and in Canada, Saturday has the highest number of readers.

Wednesday is also ad day in Canada but to a lesser extent than Saturday. Don't let the ad taker convince you to put your ad on certain days of the week. Go with what you know and what common practice is.

Bear in mind that unless people are really looking for something particular in the paper, they don't look at the paper during the week.

They are more relaxed during weekends and are likely to pick up the paper from the kitchen table. For anxious buyers however, they deliberately read the papers every morning with the hope that they find the "house of their dreams".

Would You Repeat That Please?

Once your ad is published, buy the paper and read your ad a few times, ensuring that all details are correctly listed.

Look at your phone number and make sure it was listed correctly. Do not forget to list your area code.

The same city may have two different area codes – one for the east end district and another for the west end side of town. You could lose hundreds of potential buyers with this omission.

How Do I Sound?

So the ad has been placed. Brace yourself for calls! They will increase in number as people read your ad and then pass it off to friends and family.

Rehearse your lines. You'll want to give the impression that you're a serious seller, so you expect the same from them as buyers.

Don't panic if you're getting too many calls or none at all on the first day. Take a deep breath and get ready for the avalanche. While having an answering machine is a good idea for the sake of filtering serious callers from the frivolous, it's perfectly alright for you to take the call yourself if you feel like it.

Take It Down

Have pen and paper ready. Take down each caller's name and number. Jot down their questions. This will give you an idea of future questions, and you'll know how to answer them properly the next time.

Are You A (Phone) Grouch?

When you answer calls, come across as friendly. The impression you DON'T want to give is that of a tired, harassed seller who's sick and tired of answering questions on the phone.

Practice basic courtesy. Be professional. And sound like one!

Priscilla Greene
Let's Get Serious Here

Here's an important tip: if you get 25 calls by the third day, your ad worked. Getting 25 calls means that 25 people read your ad and dialed your number.

Don't expect 25 buyers though. Callers and buyers are two separate people.

CHAPTER 7- SHOWING YOUR HOME

It Bothers Me...

When buyers come to visit, make sure there is nothing about your house that will distract them. Make sure the entrance door is clean, and if it's winter time, make sure the snow has been cleared.

Ensure that the entranceway is well lit and doesn't look in disarray. Remove coats and other clothing from their field of vision, no skis by the doorway, no ball or other play objects that may obstruct the path or cause them to trip over. A buyer who trips in your house is a terrible way to start.

Dust Collectors

Buyers must feel that the seller has taste and class. Get rid of clutter before their visit. Dust collecting trophies and souvenir items bought during trips can make an ugly sight especially if they're too close to one another without any order and are thick with dust!

Surround Yourself with Beauty

Of course be old-fashioned: good lights and flowers would be nice (not too much though – your buyer could be allergic to flower scents).

I Knew you'd Ask That!

Putting up signs to answer frequent questions can save you time. It's also an efficient way to let you give the tour without being interrupted too many times.

Signs can include things like: condo fees are $150.00 per month, appliances, fixtures and draperies are included with the sale, garage and garden equipment are included, china not included, there are 8 phone jacks on the first floor and 3 on the second floor, there is a wireless connection, shelves are included, etc.

Children OK, Animals NO!

Get your pets out of the way. You won't know in advance who is allergic to dogs and cats. Plus the barking of dogs and the meowing of cats can be very distracting, and an annoyance for non-pet lovers.

Who's That Standing by the Door?

Before buyers come, it's good to have a closer. The closer should be clearly visible to buyers, and should be near the door so he/she can keep track of buyers who arrive and leave the property.

The closer can usually tell by your instincts who are the interested buyers. When the closer asks if they want to know how the bidding process works, those who are not interested will simply say no and leave.

CHAPTER 8- NEGOTIATIONS, SETTLEMENT AND CONTRACT

Can We Talk About Your Price?

You can be 99% sure that buyers will negotiate to bring the price down; this is why houses are sold and bought as a result of negotiations, which could take days, if you're lucky, or longer, if you meet buyers who really want your house but don't want to pay the price you're asking for.

It's curious what kind of arguments buyers will come up with to convince you to lower your price. "But your backyard needs a lot of tending"; "The kitchen tiles are not in good shape and we'd have to replace them ourselves"; or "But your house is near a cemetery (or a prison or a quarry), who'd want to buy your house?"

Don't let buyers run you and your house down. If you want to unburden yourself quickly of your property because you've got an important trip scheduled or you need to make a counteroffer on another property, then by all means lower your price.

However, if you're convinced that your property is worth more (based on the offers you've received so far), then be firm with your price.

Buyers will always take advantage of those situations where you show a little hesitation about the price. Tell them your price is final and that you're not prepared to negotiate.

It Doesn't Hurt To Be Honest

When negotiations begin, remember that honesty is still the best policy. There is this great temptation to get greedy and you bid against your buyers. Don't. You may end up still owning your house months later because the bidders couldn't keep up with the price.

The more important consideration for you is not how much extra thousands of dollars you can get above your original price, but if you're a decent person, your # 1 concern should be who, among these buyers, will pay me for what I asked for and take good care of my house the way I did?

My Home Is Your Home Now

Once you've found a buyer for your home and all the terms have been negotiated to both parties' satisfaction, the next step is to transfer ownership of the house. Since you're on your own, you'll need to initiate the paper work yourself.

This is where the government can help you. The US Department of Housing and Urban Development has published a book entitled "Settlement Costs". It is free and contains valuable guidelines on settlement matters (the booklet title may have changed, check with your city government).

From this publication, you'll be able to decide who to consult with in terms of the different steps of the closing process. You will need a lawyer (or notary), or an escrow company or your bank. Settlement procedures vary from state to state and from country to country.

How Quickly Will He Settle This Matter For Me?

After you have chosen your settlement agent, get the name of the settlement agent of your buyer and provide this to your own agent.

The way it works is the two agents will then work together to contact the banks, arrange for title searches and title insurance, draw up the sale contract and calculate any other fees that have to be paid.

Settlement agents don't work with the same speed as other agents. If you feel that the process has stalled and it's not your agent's fault, then your buyer's agent may be causing the delays. If delays become major concerns, you may want to seriously consider the next buyer on your list, but inform the first buyer that you can't afford to wait any longer.

This Covers Just About Everything

When settlement details are finalized, a contract is drawn up. The contract must include the following details:

- Amount/location of property
- Timing of the sale
- Transfer of funds
- Items included in, and excluded from, the sale
- Conveyance of title
- Apportionment of fees to be paid
- Insurance matters

And other such things that are typically part of a sale contract for private property. If there are any clauses that you don't understand, have your lawyer explain them to you. Ask questions until you're satisfied that everything is crystal clear.

Can We Change This A Little Bit?

Be prepared for requests from the buyer to modify parts of the contract. Don't verbally agree to anything until your lawyer confirms that the requested changes are in order.

This part of the exercise may take longer than you expected. Lawyers are shrewd creatures and will make every attempt to get the most for their clients. They're only doing their job, and they're doing what they're best at – arguing and haggling.

It is up to your lawyer to defend your interests so hopefully, the lawyer you hired is as sharp and shrewd as your buyer's lawyer.

When contract discussions are going on, ask your lawyer's opinion as to the advantages and disadvantages of agreeing or disagreeing with a particular clause. Discuss potential consequences and how changing a clause could jeopardize your rights as a seller.

And if you do agree to change a clause, ensure that all changes are put in writing either within the body of the contract or as an addendum.

About That Money

Ask your lawyer about asking for a down payment from the buyer. Some contracts require it to protect the seller: This down payment will usually make the buyer live up to his commitment to buy the property within a reasonable amount of time.

This down payment is called "earnest money" by some people. It morally obliges the buyer to finalize a mortgage with his bank, to have the property inspected within a reasonable period and to be prepared to settle by a certain date.

This down payment is not refunded back to the buyer should the sale not take place. Down payments may range from $1,000 to as much as 10% of the purchase price and is kept in escrow by your settlement agent.

Crossing the T's And Dotting the I's

As soon as all paperwork is final and parties are ready to sign the contract, the settlement (also called closing in some parts of Canada) takes place in either of the following places: the settlement agent's office, bank, insurance office, or anywhere where you and the buyer and your respective agents agree to meet and sign papers.

This is the day you will probably get the biggest cash windfall in your life, and when someone else takes ownership of your house.

You can start breathing normally again when that check lands on your hands, and you and your personal effects are physically out of your house!

What, you've Changed Your Mind?

Expect last minute surprises. A deal can be called off because:

- The buyer could not get financing and has no money of his own,
- Something went wrong with the title search or an insurance detail was not dealt with,
- Someone suddenly is afraid and wants to back out, or
- Some personal emergencies – like a sudden death in the family or terminal illness – are forcing the parties not to go through with the deal.

Whatever happens, just make sure you're not walking up the path towards financial ruin.

You're Willing To Pay More For My House?

When you put an ad for your house, and the price looks reasonable to the pool of buyers that are out there, you'll get end buyers.

End buyers are buyers who are looking to buy a house to live in.

You'll also get professional buyers – they include real estate brokers looking for homes to buy, builders specializing in remodeling and reselling homes or developers who want to buy the property because of the land.

Don't be afraid of the professional buyers, because they know the true value of your house. They'll push the bidding price higher because they know what they're doing, and by pushing up the price, they weed off the end buyers who eventually drop out because the price is beyond their budget.

If a professional buyer offers you a price for your house that will make you happy, then by all means, go with the professional buyer.

Weeding Out the Curious

If after you place your ad, you get 100 calls, don't let that make you comfortable thinking that your house is going to be sold immediately.

The truth is, of those 100 calls, less than half are serious buyers. Or half of them want your home but don't have the means to buy it.

Of that bunch, there is only 1 truly qualified buyer, and that qualified buyer is the one who can deliver the cash when it's time to deliver it. The other 99 are just "probably" buyers.

Conclusion

These tips have served as your starter kit. You'll now need to make a decision about whether you still want to go solo. Many have done so; and after they've sold their first house, they wouldn't hesitate to do it again!

Knowledge is power, that's how the classic adage goes. And it's more meaningful when you're selling your house. Soldiers don't go to combat without orders, plans, maps and guns.

Entrepreneurs don't create businesses that will one day flourish without prior knowledge of the product or service they want to peddle.

Surgeons don't go into the operating room without knowledge of their patient – his disease and the drugs he's taking.

As a first time seller, these 101 tips are your ammunition, your basic knowledge. And it's up to you to use them to your advantage. You want this experience to be a win-win situation.

After all, part of your worth as a human being is tied to your house. Your property is a reflection of the long years of hard work and savings you've put into it.

If you're about to sell your house and the market is still hot – like it has been in the last 5-7 years – you'll have that cash windfall you've always dreamed of. Your house will make you rich. So we hope you've taken good care of it. When you sign those settlement papers, it's your house's turn to take care of you.

Good luck!

Priscilla Greene

ABOUT THE AUTHOR

One of the most important things Priscilla learned was that an attractive yard sign indicating that the home is for sale can help to draw buyers to the home. Those who come to look at the home from the sign have already seen the exterior and the neighborhood making them a more informed buyer than those responding to an online or print ad. Sellers can also buy signs with holders to provide written information on the home to prospective buyers. Learn much more useful tips inside Pricilla's book House for Sale by Owner.

www.ingramcontent.com/pod-product-compliance
Lightning Source LLC
Chambersburg PA
CBHW051252170526
45165CB00004B/1679